Richard Newton

The Present Crisis in the Protestant Episcopal Church

Richard Newton

The Present Crisis in the Protestant Episcopal Church

ISBN/EAN: 9783337380069

Printed in Europe, USA, Canada, Australia, Japan

Cover: Foto ©Lupo / pixelio.de

More available books at **www.hansebooks.com**

THE

PRESENT CRISIS

IN THE

PROTESTANT EPISCOPAL CHURCH,

AND THE

DUTY OF EVANGELICAL MEN IN REFERENCE TO IT.

BEING THE

SUBSTANCE OF A SERMON

PREACHED IN THE CHURCH OF THE EPIPHANY

BY THE RECTOR,

REV. RICHARD NEWTON, D.D.,

Philadelphia, May 31, 1874.

PUBLISHED BY REQUEST.

PHILADELPHIA:

JAMES HAMMOND,

SUCCESSOR TO THE PROTESTANT EPISCOPAL BOOK SOCIETY.

1224 CHESTNUT STREET.

1874.

THE PRESENT CRISIS

PROTESTANT EPISCOPAL CHURCH.

THE subject now to be considered is, the present crisis in the Protestant Episcopal Church, and the duty of evangelical men in reference thereto.

There *does* exist a crisis in this Church. On the one hand, there is a party in the Church that are rushing into all the extremes of sacerdotalism. They would carry the Church back to the doctrines and practices of the dark ages, before the Reformation dawned. On the other hand, there has been organized during the past year, what is called a Reformed Episcopal Church, and some very worthy and excellent persons from this Protestant Episcopal Church have joined it. And the question now before us—*the* question of the day, for evangelical men to consider is this—what is our duty in reference to this new Church? I take my stand decidedly, and firmly by the old Church, and now wish to present five good, and substantial reasons why evangelical men should not leave this Church

The first reason, and the most natural one, for not leaving the old Church is, that ITS STANDARDS OF DOCTRINE REMAIN UNALTERED.

These standards are found in the Creeds, and the Thirty-nine Articles. Taken together, these contain a body of Christian doctrine as sound and scriptural as can be found in any church on earth. They are the inheritance which we have received from our fathers. They constitute a treasure of truth wrought out from the inexhaustible mine of God's blessed word, by the labor and care of successive generations of earnest and devoted men of God. This treasure comes down to us hallowed by the prayers and tears, and sealed with the blood of confessors and martyrs. Many of the saintliest men the Church of Jesus Christ has ever known, have been indebted for their spiritual birth and growth, for all their usefulness on earth, and all their preparation for glory and bliss in heaven, to the influence and power of the truth embodied in these standards. And the truth thus enshrined, remains to-day, just as it has been for generations past, unchanged in a single feature. If these standards had been tampered with—if any efforts had been successfully made to cast poison into these fountains, so that the streams flowing from them were thoroughly corrupted, then it would be different. The instinct of self preservation, and every consideration for the honor of God, and the integrity of his truth, would require us no longer to linger by the side of streams that were hopelessly corrupt, because the fountain from which they sprung had been poisoned. But this is not so. No one can call in question this declaration. That there are difficulties with the streams we admit. To these we shall refer by and by; but the fountain of doctrine, as made up of the Creeds and Articles of the Church, continues pure.

How different it was in the Church of Rome, at the time of the Reformation! Then the fountain from which all the streams of the church's teaching flowed was radically corrupted. The Bible was a sealed book. The creeds remained in the church, indeed, but no open Bible, or scriptural standard was allowed, to show the meaning of those creeds. Tradition was their sole interpreter. It was not what God said about them, but what the Fathers said, which was to be taken into account. No man might put any construction upon them, till it had first been authorised and approved by Cardinals and Councils, by Priests and Popes. It was *this*, mainly, which led to the Reformation. If Martin Luther, and the reformers, could have had such a standard of doctrine as we have in the

Thirty-nine Articles of our Church, with an open Bible from which to defend them—and with unfettered liberty in the proclamation of them, notwithstanding the monstrous corruptions which abounded in the Church of Rome, they would have lived, and labored, and died, without a moment's thought of going off to establish a reformed church. The fountain from which the church's teaching then flowed was poisoned to its inmost recesses.

God revealed to Luther the fountain of pure truth in the Bible. If Luther and his friends had been allowed to open that fountain, close by the corrupted one that was sending its poisoned water through the Romish Church, so that the two streams might have flowed on side by side, they would have been not only content, but perfectly satisfied. They would have remained in the Church wherein they were born. But they were not allowed to do this. The mere thought of it caused the thunders of the Vatican to be hurled at their heads. The resistless arm of Papal power was stretched forth to hinder them from opening the fountain of living waters, anywhere within the limits of the Church of Rome. It was nothing but *this* which took them out of that Church. They did not voluntarily go out, they were driven out. And if Martin Luther were here to-day, clearly understanding

the state of things in this troubled Church of ours,
I feel perfectly assured that he would endorse this
first point of my argument, and say to evangelical
men everywhere, " It is a good and sufficient reason
why you should not leave your Church, that its
doctrinal standards remain pure and uncorrupted."

*But, secondly, evangelical men ought not to leave
the Church in her present difficulties*, BECAUSE AS
FAITHFUL SERVANTS OF CHRIST, OUR DUTY REQUIRES
US NOT TO RUN AWAY FROM ERROR, BUT TO STAND
FIRM IN OUR PLACE, AND MANFULLY OPPOSE IT.

This is especially true of the *ministers* in the
Church. I have been asked a score of times or
more, since this new movement took place, why I
have not joined it? My reply to this is, that "I
believe I was inwardly moved by the Holy Ghost"
to enter the ministry of this Church. I *know* I
have never been so moved to go out of it; and
until the same voice which called me into the
office I now occupy shall bid me go out of it, I
cannot for one moment think of doing so.

Before his admission to the office of Presbyter
in this Church, every minister records his solemn
vow before God, that "he will be ready with all
faithful diligence to banish and drive away from
the Church all erroneous and strange doctrines
contrary to God's word." Now this vow binds me

to duty at the post where God in his providence has placed me, and not at any other place on this round earth to which I may choose to go.

But, if we wish to oppose error successfully, we must not run away from it, and get as far as possible out of its reach; but put ourselves in the closest contact with it; we must stand up to it, shoulder to shoulder, and foot to foot, and flash the light of God's blessed truth, clear and strong on every distorted lineament of its hideous features. The light is needed most where darkness is the thickest. Salt is of no use in places where there is no danger of corruption and decay. Suppose that you and I were entering a village in which we knew that a fatal disease, like the plague, was prevailing. A little distance from the village we meet with the principal physician of the place. He has gathered all his remedies together, and is fleeing from the disease-infected district. We ask him what he means by leaving the village? His reply is: " I have been struggling with the disease as long as I thought there was any prospect of success. But now I am satisfied that further effort will be unavailing. It is impossible to make headway against it, and so I am going to retire to some healthy position where I shall be beyond the reach of this terrible malady." What should we think of such a man? What would the brethren of his profession—noble-minded, high-toned men as they are—think of such conduct? Is not this a fair illustration of the case we are considering?

Take another illustration. Suppose that you and I are officers on board of a United States frigate on a voyage round the world. We are bound in honor to protect the property of our government, and the flag which represents it. In the course of the voyage we find that there is a mutiny among some of the officers and crew. They have united together in the attempt to haul down the old flag, and get possession of the vessel, and either run her ashore, or hand her over to the enemies of our government. We make head against the mutineers for awhile; but not succeeding to our satisfaction, we get discouraged, and resolve to give up the contest; or rather we make up our minds to transfer the scene of our further efforts for the interest and honor of our government. We put some spare spars together and make a raft; we climb over the side of the vessel, and leave the old flag to be hauled down by the mutineers, and the vessel, the property of our government we leave wholly in their power. We may indeed erect a pole on our raft, and unfurl the flag upon it, and claim still to be faithful to it, and its interests. But is it so? Let us put this question to any right-minded officer of the navy. His eye will flash, and his cheek will burn with honest indignation at the mere thought of such a thing. And his instant earnest response will be: " No! No! '*Don't give up the ship!*' Plant yourselves on her quarter-deck, beneath ' the star spangled banner' you have sworn to defend. There stand, and fight like men. And if you must fall—then fall at your post—and with the flag of your country still waving over you."

If the mutineers overpower us, and we are driven from the ship, against our will, and by a power we are unable to resist, then the fault is not ours. But as faithful servants of the government that has sent us forth, while we have an arm to use, or an energy to put forth, we are solemnly bound to use that arm, and put forth that energy on board the old ship, and under the old flag.

And just so it should be with evangelical men in their relation to the old Protestant Episcopal Church. Faithfulness to our Master requires us to stand up manfully at the posts He has assigned us, and serve Him there as best we may. In the position we occupy in this Church we have an opportunity of delivering our testimony to God's truth, just where that testimony is more needed, and where it will be more effectual for good, than in any other place we could occupy on the face of this earth. Here we can contend for Episcopacy as an historical fact, while denying and opposing with all our might the arrogant, and exclusive claims of some of its advocates. There is one short argument that quietly, but effectually disposes of these claims. It is this: that under the Jewish dispensation, when God desired to have an exclusive priestly succession in the family of Aaron, He made His will so plain respecting it, by statements both positive and negative, that the question was settled, beyond dispute, through all the subsequent history of that nation. And if God had designed that there should be in the Christian Church a similar succession from the Apostles, exclusive and actual, He could have made His will concerning it just as plain and clear in this case, as it was in the former. He did this in the Jewish Church when He wanted a succession; and it is but reasonable to suppose that He would have done the same in the Christian Church, if He had desired a succession here. But the significant, and undeniable fact is that He has *not* done so. The inference is irresistible, that it was not His will there should be any such succession.

Here we have the apostolical succession in a nut-shell. Yet the argument is one that cannot be fairly gainsaid or refuted. And there is no position under heaven where an argument like this can be used with such telling power, against the error it is designed to counteract, as that which is occupied by evangelical men in the Protestant Episcopal Church. Why should we throw away such a vantage ground for opposing error?

And, then, in our position in this Church we can contend for plain, honest tables, instead of altars in our chancels. We can denounce and oppose as idolatrous, the practice of always kneeling towards the communion table, as though the God of the Christian sanctuary were a *local* Deity, more really present in that one spot than any other in his temple. And in opposing these two dogmas, we are opposing two of the most fruitful sources from which Ritualistic error springs, with all its dangerous practices. And the place in which to do this most effectually, is not in any new Church organization, but in the old Church. We should not leave our place in this old Church, because here, better than anywhere else, we can bear our testimony against the prevailing errors of the day, and aid most efficiently in spreading abroad the precious truth of the Gospel of the Son of God.

But, in the third place, we should not leave our position in this old Church, BECAUSE IN ANY OTHER NOW EXISTING, OR ANY LIKELY TO BE ORGANIZED, WE ARE SURE TO FIND, IN ONE FORM OR OTHER, DIFFICULTIES QUITE AS GREAT AS THOSE WHICH WE HAVE NOW TO BEAR.

No form of Church organization is given us in the New Testament. All those now existing are of human origin. They bear the marks of human infirmity. Imperfection, in one form or other, clings to them all. We never shall see a perfect Church on earth till our Lord returns from heaven to make one. In each of the denominations around us I could readily point out something which it would be harder far for me to bear than anything that I meet with in my own Church.

And, in illustration of this remark, let me say that, during a ministry of well nigh forty years in this city, I have had ministerial brethren of all the leading denominations—men occupying the very first positions in their several ecclesiastical bodies—and men of the highest Christian character, at whose feet I would have been glad to take my place as a learner—I say, I have had such brethren come to me, and, in the sacred confidence of fraternal Christian fellowship, speak sorrowfully, each one for himself, of some peculiar burden,

2

under which he groaned in his own denomination, and express the earnest, longing wish that
the way had been open for him to transfer his
ecclesiastical relations, and spend the rest of his
days among the evangelical clergy of the Protestant Episcopal Church. This is a very significant
fact, but it *is* a fact.

If I were permitted to make a Church that
would be, in every particular, just what I should
desire to have it, no doubt I should be able to
please myself exactly. But then, the Church
that suited me so completely would probably not
suit my neighbor at all; and if he, in turn,
should mould and make a Church just to please
himself, you and I would be very apt to find
some grave objections in that which he esteemed
to be about perfect.

In the accounts, which the papers recently fur-
nished, of the revision of the Prayer-Book by the
Council of the Reformed Church in New York,
it would be difficult to find two persons who
would entirely agree about any of the alterations
proposed and effected there, unless, perhaps, it
might be as to the omission of the word " regenerate" in the service for infant baptism. This is
a consideration of great moment. Certainly it
should " give us pause; and lead us rather to

bear the ills we have, than flee to others that we
know not of."

*In the fourth place, evangelical men ought not to
leave their position in the Protestant Episcopal
Church* BECAUSE OF THE LIBERTY WHICH THEY HERE
ENJOY.

This is the most important reason bearing on
this subject, and the one that is least understood.
There is no man in this land, or in any other on
which the sun shines, who has more unfettered
freedom to preach the precious gospel of Jesus, in
all its simplicity and fulness, than every minister
has in this Protestant Episcopal Church of ours.
If Luther, or the Reformers, had possessed a tithe
of such liberty, they never would have dreamed of
establishing a reformation outside of the Church
in which they were born and brought up. This
liberty of preaching no one can deny or call in
question. But our brethren who have joined the
Reformed Church say, " Yes, this is true; liberty
of preaching you have; but we want liberty in
other things, which is denied to us." Let us
look at these.

" We want," say these brethren, " the liberty
of freely acknowledging the ministry of other denominations as valid and true." Now, as a matter of *doctrine*, we have this liberty to its fullest

extent. In the preface to the Prayer-Book "the different religious denominations of Christians" are distinctly spoken of as constituting "their respective Churches." Thus, at the very opening of the Prayer-Book, we find an acknowledgment of other Churches than our own. But, according to the teachings of this very book, as elsewhere given, there cannot be a Church where there is not a valid ministry, and duly administered sacraments; so that, in admitting the existence of "other Churches," we are fairly warranted in maintaining that the Prayer-Book admits the validity of the ministry and sacraments as found in those Churches. This is an honest, fair, logical deduction, and the force of it cannot be controverted.

And then look at the 23d Article of this Church. This refers to the ordination of ministers. It declares that no man is to be allowed to take upon him the office of a minister until he be "lawfully called and sent to execute the same." And then it goes on to define what ordination is, in general, in these words: "*And those we ought to judge lawfully called and sent, who be chosen and called to this work, by men who have public authority given unto them in the congregation to call and send ministers into the Lord's vineyard.*"

Now bear in mind that these Articles are the highest source of authority in matters of doctrine, in our Church, outside of the Bible. It is through the Articles that the voice of the Church is heard speaking in the most authoritative and majestic tones. And here the Church defines what ordination is *without the mention of Bishops or Episcopacy, or an apostolical succession.*

Bishop Burnet, whose work on the Articles is of the highest authority, on this subject, both in this country and in England, expressly says, when commenting on this 23d Article, that the peculiar phraseology of it was employed on purpose, so as not to exclude the Reformers on the Continent, who had not received episcopal ordination. Thus, both the history of this Article, and the express language of it combine to settle the teaching of our Church on this subject. The highest doctrinal authority in the Church declares the validity of non-episcopal orders. It is clear from this showing that evangelical men, with liberal views of the ministry, are the only true exponents of the standard teaching of our Church in the matter of orders; and *that the men who deny the validity of non-episcopal orders are really and truly not in conformity with the doctrine of the Protestant Episcopal Church on this subject.*

2*

Bishop Hopkins, of Vermont, in his reply to Milner, author of " The End of Controversy," vol. 2, p. 3, says:—

" Dr. Milner asserts that the Church of England unchurches all other Protestant communities which are without the succession of Bishops; whereas, not only Hooker, whom he quotes, but all the Reformers, with Jewell, Andrews, Usher, Bramall, and, in a word, the whole of our standard divines, agree in maintaining that Episcopacy is not necessary to the being, but only to the well-being of the Church; and they grant the name of Churches to all denominations of Christians who hold the fundamental doctrines of the Gospel, notwithstanding the imperfection and irregularity of their ministry."

Dr. C. H. Wharton, of Burlington, New Jersey, one of the chief revisers of the Amer. Prayer-Book, says:—

" The pretence of tracing up the Roman Church to the times of the Apostles, is grounded on mere sophistry. The succession which the Roman Catholics unfairly ascribe to their own Church belongs to every other, and exclusively to none. But that portion of the Christian Church is best entitled to this claim which teaches in the greatest purity the doctrine of the Apostles." St. Ambrose says, "They have not the inheritance of Peter, who have not Peter's faith," vol. 2, p. 213.

Archbishop Musgrave, of York, in 1842, says in his charge: "You would exceed all just bounds, if you insist on the Apostolical succession as the only security for the efficiency of the sacraments, so that those who do not receive them from men so accredited, are left to uncovenanted mercy. This would be to set up a claim which neither Scripture nor the formularies and various offices of our Church, nor the writings of her best divines, nor the common-sense of mankind will allow. The being and the well-being of a Church is a wide distinction, which good sense and Christian charity should ever keep in sight."—GALLAGHER'S IRENICON.

But it may be said that in the preface to the Ordinal, when about to make provision for the ordination of her own ministers, our Church takes different ground from this. Here she affirms the fact of an historical Episcopacy. She maintains that a threefold order of the ministry has always existed, and she provides that no other ministers than those of this order shall be received as regular ministers " *in this Church.*" But then there is no conflict, or contradiction between the Ordinal

and the Article here. The Article gives the defi-
nition of ordination in general, as held by the
founders of our Church ; while the Ordinal only
prescribes the particular form of ordination which
" *this Church*" prefers to have established within
her own borders. I can plant myself, honestly
and squarely on the ground of this 23d Article,
and proclaim of every Presbyterian, Methodist,
Baptist, Lutheran, or other minister in this land,
who has been " chosen and called to this work by
men who have public authority given unto them
in the congregation to call and send ministers
into the Lord's vineyard," that he is a true and
valid minister of the Lord Jesus Christ. And I
can proclaim this, not as my individual opinion,
but as the teaching of the highest doctrinal authority in the Protestant Episcopal Church in
these United States. Surely this is liberty enough
in reference to the acknowledgment of the validity
of ministers in other denominations.

But it is said, " Yes, this is so ; yet we wish
for more liberty in regard to our intercourse with
our ministerial brethren of other Churches. Our
liberty, in this respect, is too much restricted by
the canon which prohibits any but espiscopally
ordained ministers from ever officiating in our
Church."

This is undoubtedly the operation of Canon XI., Tit. I. I regret, as much as any one can, the existence of this canon. I have protested against it from the day of its enactment. I shall continue to protest against it till I die, or till it is repealed, which I am just as sure will eventually be the case as I am sure that "truth is mighty, and must prevail" in the end. But still, as a law-abiding, order-loving man, I submit to the canon. And I do so with the less regret because every one knows that a canon teaches no doctrine. All that it can do is to prescribe some rule of order or discipline. And that is the whole effect of this narrow and unchristian canon of which we are now speaking. It leaves all uncontradicted and uncontrolled the grand, broad, scriptural teaching of the 23d Article, the highest doctrinal authority in our Church on the subject of a valid ministry.

But it is said, again, that evangelical men ought to go out of the Protestant Episcopal Church because, while reasonable liberty is denied to them, the most unreasonable liberty is allowed to Ritualists and Romanists to do as they please; and that the only way to get rid of the responsibility of seeming to sustain these growing errors is to separate from them.

That the growth of error in this direction has been fearful of late years cannot be denied; that something should be done to check the progress of this error all must admit. Just what is the best and wisest way of doing it is not so easy to say. We may well pray, in the language of the Collect, that, in reference to this matter, God may give to the members of the approaching General Convention "a right judgment in all things; that they may both perceive and know what things they ought to do, and also may have grace and power faithfully to perform the same." Ritualism must and will be restrained, or else we must alter our title as a Protestant Church.

But I wish to say a word or two, under this branch of our subject, in relation to the question of individual responsibility as to the prevalence of the errors in question.

Most of those who have joined the new Church have had much to say about the burden of responsibility which they have felt on this subject. Now there are two mistakes which these brethren have made. When we do our duty in faithfully setting forth the truth, it is a mistake to suppose that God will hold us responsible for the growth of error over which we have no control. God is not a hard master. He does not deal with men in any such way as this. No one can deplore the growth of ritualist errors in our Church more earnestly than I do. But, while doing all I honestly can to oppose these errors, I feel perfectly assured that not a feather's weight of responsibility rests with me in reference to them.

The other mistake, which these brethren make in deserting their old Church, is in imagining that what God requires of them is to escape from the presence of error, rather than to stand up in manly opposition to it. But this is not so. Does a general send his soldiers into the field for the purpose of looking around, and finding for themselves snug quarters where they can settle down in peace, and have a good, quiet time, away from the inconvenience and annoyance connected with the presence of their enemies? No. But he sends them there for the very purpose of finding out where the enemy has entrenched himself in the greatest strength. Just there he would have his soldiers plant themselves. Just there he would have them charge upon the foe, and shower blows upon them thick and fast, and *keep on doing so to the end of the contest*. If the fact of being in the same Church with errorists makes me responsible for their errors, the fact of being in the same community with them must do so too. If I must leave my Church on this ground, then I must leave the city where they dwell—the country, and the world in which they are found, and what will be the end of it? If we are responsible for their errors because the same Church organization embraces us, then we must be equally responsible because we tread the same earth, and breathe the same air, and are warmed by the same sun, and have the same broad arch of heaven stretching its beautiful blue canopy over us. There is no truth or reality in any such idea.

But after all the greatest practical difficulty experienced by those who have gone out from us into the Reformed Church, remains yet to be noticed. It is the use of the word "regenerate" in the service for Infant Baptism. There is probably not an individual—among the clergy, at least—of those who have joined the new Church, who has not been impelled to take this course by the burden put upon his conscience in the use of this phrase. And this is no new difficulty; but one of old standing. The experience of generations has proved that it is *just here* that the harness of the Church's service has always galled the most. Many indeed have worked in this harness without the experience of any difficulty. But the

six or eight different views which other good men
have attempted to put upon this service, bear sad
and solemn witness to the agony of conscience
under which they have gone writhing in their
efforts to find some relief in the use of this word.
And there are numbers of earnest and faithful men,
all over the Church now, who are only enabled to
remain at their posts, and go on with their work,
by ceasing to use this word.

And I argue that evangelical men should not
leave the old Church *because they have a right to
exercise this liberty.* I argue this right on *four*
grounds:—

*In the first place there is no law in the Prostestant
Episcopal Church, in this country, binding the clergy
to a literal and verbal use of all the offices of the
Church.* It was very different in the Church of
England. Here, in the year 1662, what is known
as "The Act of Uniformity," was established.
This Act prescribed as follows:—

" That every beneficed clergyman shall declare
his unfeigned assent and consent to the use of all
things in the said book contained and prescribed,
in these words, and in no other:"—

" I, A. B., do hereby declare my unfeigned assent and consent to all and everything contained

3

and prescribed in the book entitled the Book of Common Prayer."

Now, the natural effect of such a law as this would be to give a cast-iron rigidity to the use of all the services of the Church, where it was in operation. The omission of any word, or sentence, in any offices of the Church would be a sin, because it would be " the transgression of a law" which the clergyman had solemnly bound himself to keep. And if this "Act of Uniformity" had ever been adopted in the Protestant Episcopal Church in this country, or if anything of a similar nature had ever been adopted instead of it, then it would have been wrong for any minister to omit a single word or sentence from any office of the Prayer Book. But this is not the case. *There is no such law ;* and where there is no law, there can be no transgression. The existence for generations in the Church of England of a law like this Act of Uniformity, would naturally and necessarily give rise to the feeling that it was a wrong thing, a breach of law, to omit any word in the Prayer-Book. And when the Prayer-Book came into use in this country, the same feeling would naturally be connected with it. It was the atmosphere which had gathered round it, and came with it. But the thing for us to remember is that

the law which there required this strict, unbending uniformity in the verbal use of the Prayer-
Book is not a law with us, and therefore, that
which would have been an offence to those bound
by this law, is no offence at all where this law does
not exist. This is the first point in the argument
for the liberty now asserted.

*In the second place the only obligation by which
any minister of this Church binds himself to the use
of the Prayer-Book is the Declaration which he signs
at the time of his ordination.* This declaration is
in these words:—

"I do believe the Holy Scriptures of the Old
and New Testament to be the Word of God, and
to contain all things necessary to salvation; and I
do solemnly engage to conform to the Doctrines
and Worship of the Protestant Episcopal Church
in the United States."

This is the only restraining law, that exists in
the Episcopal Church in this country, to govern
ministers in the use of the Prayer-Book. This is
all that we have here in place of the "Act of
Uniformity" that was so long the law of the Church
of England. But the poles of the earth are not
wider apart than are the requirements of that unbending, adamantine, and monstrously oppressive
"Act of Uniformity," on the one hand, and those

of this simple, sensible, general, flexible, and most liberal declaration which our Church requires of her ministers, on the other. Conformity to the Doctrines and Worship of the Church—this is all to which any minister of this Church has pledged himself. This is the extent to which the law reaches by which he is bound. But he conforms to the doctrines of the Church so long as his teachings are in harmony with the Creeds and Articles of the Church. He conforms to the worship of the Church so long as he uses, on the stated occasions of public service in the sanctuary, the order of worship which this Church has appointed. Honestly and fairly interpreted, *this is all to which the declaration in question binds a minister*, and therefore this is all for which he can justly be held responsible.

This is the second point in the argument for the liberty here claimed.

In the third place, as a matter of fact, it is a simple, but undeniable truth, that a liberty of this kind has always been allowed in this Church.

I refer, in proof of this statement, to the general practice in regard to the use of the Office for the Visitation of the sick. This is one of the appointed " occasional offices" of this Church, just as the office for Infant Baptism is. They are found side by side in the Prayer-Book, among its occasional offices. The Rubrics are as absolute and peremptory in the one office as in the other. They both stand on the same ground of obligation; the authority which requires me to use the office for the visitation of the sick is precisely the same authority which requires me to use the office for the baptism of infants. It is neither more nor less in the one case than in the other; yet I have never used the office for the visitation of the sick as it stands in the Prayer-Book, in the whole course of my ministry, and I never expect to do so. I have occasionally used some of the beautiful prayers in that service, and been thankful for them; but as for the rest of that office *I have always omitted it.* And this I presume has been, in substance, the practice of every minister in this Church, from the oldest bishop to the youngest deacon; and yet no one has ever thought of asking the authority of the General Convention for liberty to make omissions in that service. And nobody ever dreams that the men, who are doing this all the time, are failing in their duty, and breaking the law which binds them to conformity with the worship of the Protestant Episcopal Church. Now, if a man, without any failure of duty or breach of law, may omit the whole, or the greater part, of

3*

one of the occasional offices of, the Church, then surely he cannot be chargeable with failure of duty, or breach of law, for omitting a *single phrase*, or *sentence*, in another of these offices. Where the liberty exists to do the greater thing, the liberty to do the less must exist also.

But the fourth point in this argument is the strongest and most conclusive of all, viz., that every minister is bound to the exercise of just such a liberty as this by his ordination vow.

When I was admitted to the office of Presbyter in this Church, the Bishop proposed to me these questions: "Are you persuaded that the Holy Scriptures contain all doctrine required as necessary for eternal salvation? And are you determined, out of the said Scriptures, to instruct the people committed to your charge, and to teach nothing as necessary to eternal salvation but that which you shall be persuaded may be concluded and proved by the Scriptures?"

To these questions the answer given was:—

" I *am* so persuaded, and *have* so determined by the grace of God."

Now, in this part of the ordination service this Church puts an open Bible, into the hands of every man who enters her ministry, and solemnly swears him to the exercise of his own private judgment, on the truths of that book, as the rule by which he is to be guided in all that he teaches. If any should argue that this only refers to the sermons the minister may preach from the pulpit, but that it cannot be intended to apply to the language which the Church has introduced into her own services, I answer that if *preaching* were the word here used, there would be force in this argument; but it is not so. It runs thus: "Are you determined to *teach* nothing but that which you shall be persuaded may be concluded and proved by Scripture." This ordination vow, therefore, throws the minister back upon his own conscience, enlightened by the Scriptures, as the rule by which he is to be guided in all the language he employs in teaching the people, whether it be in the sermons he preaches, or the services that he performs in other parts of his public duty. It must necessarily mean this. To deny it, is to suppose that the Church intended to bind a solemn vow on the consciences of her ministers, which must place them, at times, in the most painful and trying dilemmas.

For example, suppose that I stand in my place in the pulpit, and preach to my people on some such text as this: "Of his own will begat He us by the word of truth." I show from these words

that the subject here treated of, is that of the
soul's conversion, or, of spiritual regeneration, and
that the instrument which God has ordained for
the accomplishment of this work is the word of
truth.

After this service is over I go to the font and
baptise a child. The baptism is completed. Then
I stand up and say, " seeing now that this child is
regenerated, etc.;" and then engaging in prayer, I
say, " We yield Thee hearty thanks, most merciful
Father, that it hath pleased Thee to regenerate this child by Thy Holy Spirit, etc." At the
conclusion of this service an intelligent member
of my congregation comes up to me and says, "I
am greatly perplexed in regard to this matter of
spiritual regeneration. In the pulpit you teach
me one thing about it from the Bible; and then
at the font you give me entirely different teaching
about it from the Prayer-Book. Which of these
two teachings must I believe?"

This is a very serious dilemma to be placed in.
I find I am teaching my people in the pulpit one
thing about spiritual regeneration which " I am
persuaded *can* be proved from Scripture;" and
then, at the font, I am teaching them another
thing about it which I am persuaded *cannot* be
proved from Scripture. Yet there is that solemn

vow staring me in the face all the while; what must I do? I must omit the word regenerate, because whatever construction I may put upon it in my own mind—and there is no difficulty in doing this satisfactorily—yet experience proves that the word cannot be used without the danger of teaching what I am persuaded cannot be proved from Scripture. *My ordination vow compels me to do this; while the declaration which I have signed, of conformity to the worship of this Church, does not, in any fair, and honest interpretation, interfere with my doing it.*

This is my argument for the liberty here claimed in regard to the baptismal service. I believe it to be a perfectly sound and logical argument; and this being so, it follows necessarily, that the liberty here claimed is *an inherent and inalienable liberty.* I cannot ask the General Convention to grant this liberty, because it already belongs, of right, to all who feel called upon to exercise it. I do not say this in any factious or rebellious spirit; I claim to be a thoroughly law-abiding, order-loving minister of the Church to which I belong. I only wish to get down to the solid rock, on which the law of liberty legitimately rests; I believe, honestly before God, that the argument here used places this law fairly on that rock.

But, it may be said that, in some parts of the Church, the man who takes this ground would be presented for trial. Very well, suppose that such should be the case. A presents B for trial, because he omits a word, or sentence, in one of the offices of the Church. What is to prevent B from turning round, and presenting A in turn for trial, on the ground that he omits the whole, or the greater part, of another of the Church's offices; and when A shows where he gets his authority for the larger omission, B will not have far to go for his authority for the smaller omission. Now A and B, we suppose, are both on trial. In conducting their trial they ask—what of course would be too reasonable to be denied—that the principle which our blessed Lord laid down be applied to their case, when He said, "Let him that is without sin among you," *i. e.*, a similar sin of omission, "cast the first stone at them;" and if you travel through the Church, from one end of it to the other, you will not find *one man*, who, on this principle, will be competent to engage in trying A and B; not one who can lay his hand on his breast and say honestly before God, "I never have omitted as much, from any office of the Church, as these two brethren are charged with omitting, and I here solemnly promise that I never will do so." No man living in the Church can say this. And how, then will this matter end? It will soon end, in such an understanding of the real merits of the case, that we shall all come to see, that no choice is left us, between going back to the old English law of unbending uniformity, on the one hand, or freely admitting the law of liberty here contended for, on the other.

It may be objected again that the admission of such a principle as this would lead to confusion and disorder, and mar the harmony of our worship.

The natural reply here is, that this principle has already been admitted, and acted on, in reference to one of the offices of the Church, and no such evil has arisen from it. And so it would be here. Suppose, for example, that some minister is found omitting one or more of the opening sentences of the Litany, refering to the doctrine of the Trinity: could he plead the principle now contended for, to justify him in that course? Certainly not. For in such omission he fails of conformity with the doctrine of the Church; and if he cannot conform to that doctrine he must leave the Church. And so with any other word or sentence that touches the doctrine of the Church. It is clear that we can admit the operation of the principle of liberty here refered to, and yet have all the safeguard that is needed, in the law which binds us to conformity with the doctrines and worship of the Church. A liberty which interferes with these cannot be allowed. The liberty which leaves these untouched *is already granted, and cannot be withdrawn.*

And so I say that evangelical men ought not to leave the Church, because of the liberty which they have in it.

But, lastly, I maintain that evangelical men should not leave the old Church, BECAUSE THE MULTIPLICATION OF DENOMINATIONS IS AN EVIL SO GREAT, AND GRIEVOUS THAT NOTHING CAN JUSTIFY IT, BUT THE MOST ABSOLUTE NECESSITY.

It leads to strife and contention, and bitterness and wrath, and a train of endless evils. These evils are not felt so much in our large cities. But they are seen and felt, with all their sad results, in the smaller towns and villages of our country. Every Christian man, who has lived in one of these places, has been made to mourn in real, heartfelt sorrow, over the manifold evils that spring out of the numerous, and unnecessary different Church organizations, that are struggling for a precarious existence there. And shall we help to increase these evils, by adding still another to the too numerous sects and parties already in existence?

Think what a vast amount of money, that might be directly employed in alleviating the wants of the sick and the suffering, in reclaiming the wandering, and saving the lost, is now worse than wasted in building higher the walls of division, and drawing deeper the lines of separation between Christian brethren! And shall we open another outlet for unholy waste in this direction? Think of the wealth and the working machinery, and the many noble institutions of this grand, old, historical Church of ours; and shall we evangelical men, go out, and leave her, with all her institutions, and all her multiplied agencies for good, in the control of a party who are seeking to unprotestantise the Church, and overturn the very foundation on which she rests? How shall we answer it to our Master, if we do? When He shall point to the scattered and neglected flocks, on whom we voluntarily, and unnecessarily turned our backs, and address to us the solemn, searching question, "with whom did ye leave those few sheep in the wilderness?" what shall we say? No, for the good and substantial reasons now given, I believe that the duty of evangelical men in the Protestant Episcopal Church is not to go out from her, but to stand manfully by her, in the trying crisis through which she is now passing.

In conclusion, let me say that, if the views here set forth, had been taken in our Church, years ago, we never should have heard of the Reformed Church which has been started during the past year. And if the principle of liberty here claimed is only allowed and exercised, then there is no presumption in asserting that the days of this Reformed Church are numbered. The supposed necessity for its existence will have passed away, and those who have joined its ranks will soon be found returning to their old places. With this principle of liberty allowed we shall need no revision of the Prayer-Book. Not a line of it need be altered. We shall not require even the alternate phrases of which we have heard so much. The old Book may stand as it has always stood. We need not mar its beauty by any erasures. We do not strike out, or enclose in brackets, those portions of the office for the visitation of the sick which nobody uses, but we let them stand as they have always stood. And so let it be with the office for Infant Baptism. There are many men in the Church who find no difficulty in the use of the term "regenerate" in this service. Let them go on and use it. There are other men *who would rather lay down their lives* than be compelled to use this term; let them omit it. This breaks no law. It subverts no authority. It introduces no new principle. It only makes another application of a principle that has always been allowed. This principle lies embedded in the granite rock on which the constitution of our Church is based. The two pillars on which this principle rests— pillars that never can be shaken while the Church stands—are the declaration which every minister signs at the time of his ordination, and the ordination vow to which I have referred.

This principle allowed will give to our Church that element of flexibility on the one hand, and comprehensiveness on the other, which are imperatively demanded, if she is to go forward with success and do the great work for the glory of God, and for the good of men which I believe she is designed to do.

And believing this to be the only true way in which to solve the problem of our present difficulties, I say frankly here, that I hope the General Convention will make no changes in the Prayer-Book. Memorials to this effect no doubt will be presented there. They will be read, of course, with the respect which is due to the right of petition; but there I trust the matter will be allowed to rest. What we need, in order to secure the best interests of our Church, is not authority from the General

Convention to do this thing, or to leave that thing undone; it is simply to understand clearly the law of liberty wherewith Christ and this Church have made us free; and faithfully, and as in the sight of God, to use that liberty.

I have been regarded during all the days of my ministerial life as a strong party man. And this, I am free to confess is the simple truth. In times of strife and division, men with clear, strong views of doctrine and duty, must take ground on one side or other, in reference to the questions that are at issue. But with the mellowing influence of advancing years I find myself caring less and less for the views of any party, but more and more for the great interest and welfare of the Church that I love. The utterances here made are not the promptings of any spirit of party. That God who searcheth the hearts and trieth the reins of the children of men is my witness, that I have said nothing on this occasion but what I sincerely believe will tend to promote the best and enduring interests of this Church. I have only given expression now, for the first time in public, to thoughts and convictions that have been long maturing in my own mind, and have been pondered and prayed over for years. The best years and energies of my life and heart have been given

to the welfare of this Church; and in her service
I hope to spend whatever of strength or life remains to me. It grieves me to the heart when I
hear of one, and another, of those I love, forsaking
a Church in which they hear the gospel of Jesus
preached, in its simplicity and fulness, and where
they have the most unfettered freedom to work
for God, and to worship Him, that mortal men
can desire. In doing this I cannot but think they
are making a mistake; and yet it is not in my
heart to give utterance to one unkind or reproach-
ful word towards them. This dear old Church has
passed through many periods of darkness and difficulty in the past. But God has always watched
over and kept her hitherto, and I believe He will
watch over and keep her still. She has weathered
many a storm before, and I feel confident that she
will weather that which is now bursting upon her,
and causing every timber in her venerable frame,
from stem to stern, to tremble. I believe that the
dark clouds now gathering round her will break,
and roll away; and that she will come out from
this overshadowing gloom, "clear as the sun, fair
as the moon, beautiful as Tirzah, comely as Jeru-
salem, and terrible as an army with banners."

There is one of our sweet hymns written by one
who belonged to another denomination from our

own. We are all accustomed to sing it in reference to the Church universal. We are also wont to apply it to our own branch of that universal Church. As expressive of the deepest feeling of my heart to this dear old Church, in these days of her sore trial, I close by saying, in the words of this hymn:—

" I love thy Church, O God ;
   Her walls before thee stand,
Dear as the apple of thine eye,
   And graven on thy hand.

If e'er my heart forget
   Her welfare, or her woe,
Let every joy this heart forsake,
   And every grief o'erflow.

For her my tears shall fall ;
   For her my prayers ascend ;
To her my cares and toils be given,
   Till toils and cares shall end."

www.ingramcontent.com/pod-product-compliance
Lightning Source LLC
Chambersburg PA
CBHW021445090426

42739CB00009B/1645